Sight Words

This workbook belongs to

W9-CTH-328

Use pencils, crayons, and stickers to complete the activities in this book. When there is a sticker missing, you will see this pattern:

Color it.   Trace it.   Write it.

Color it.	Trace it.	Write it.
me	me	
we	we	
he	he	
she	she	

Here **we** are.

Whisper it.	me	we	he	she
Say it.	me	we	he	she
Clap it.	me	we	he	she

Word art

Use the key to finish coloring the picture.

me = orange   we = blue   he = green   she = red

Sight words 2

Color it. Trace it. Write it.

no	no	
yes	yes	
to	to	
like	like	

He said **yes**.

She said **no**.

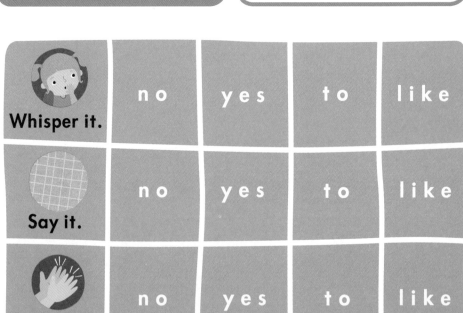

Whisper it.	no	yes	to	like
Say it.	no	yes	to	like
Clap it.	no	yes	to	like

Word maze

Follow the word **like** to help the rabbits reach the carrots.

Start

Finish

Sight words ③

Color it.	Trace it.	Write it.
and	and	
for	for	
but	but	
with	with	

This is **for** you.

	and	for	but	with
Whisper it.	and	for	but	with
Say it.	and	for	but	with
Clap it.	and	for	but	with

Find the word

Circle the word that is spelled correctly in each row.

dna (and) nad dan

rof orf for rfor

but bot bul ubt

wiht witt whit with

Sight words 4

Color it. Trace it. Write it.

Color it.	Trace it.	Write it.
so	so	
can	can	
now	now	
said	said	

I **can** do it **now**.

	so	can	now	said
Whisper it.	so	can	now	said
Say it.	so	can	now	said
Clap it.	so	can	now	said

Count the words

Help Pippa count the words. Write the numbers in the boxes.
Circle the word that appears most often.

so **8**   can ☐   now ☐   said ☐

so can can now
so can now
so can so now
now so said so
said can so
now now now
said now
so so now
now now
can said

Sight words 5

Color it. Trace it. Write it.

Color it.	Trace it.	Write it.
do	do	
has	has	
had	had	
have	have	

She **has** a balloon.

	do	has	had	have
Whisper it.	do	has	had	have
Say it.	do	has	had	have
Clap it.	do	has	had	have

Word search

Help Harry find each sight word in the word search.

do ✓   has ✓   had ✓   have ✓

a d e m a i g e p
h o e h a d a o a
m e u s h e d r h
h u e a u h a s a
a a v e d a o e e
v m v a e s
e s a i b a
a v o s d v

Sight words 6

Color it. Trace it. Write it.

the	the	
they	they	
this	this	
that	that	

They like **this** dog.

Whisper it.	the	they	this	that
Say it.	the	they	this	that
Clap it.	the	they	this	that

Link the letters

Help Eve find and link the letters to spell the words.

the they this that

h i u t h e t j

t t h a t a h

t b

t h e y h

a x i

h t h s

t

w o m

Color it. Trace it. Write it.

Color it	Trace it	Write it
why	why	
who	who	
what	what	
when	when	

Who is that?

Whisper it.	why	who	what	when
Say it.	why	who	what	when
Clap it.	why	who	what	when

Word art

Use the key to finish coloring the picture.

why = yellow   who = purple   what = blue   when = red

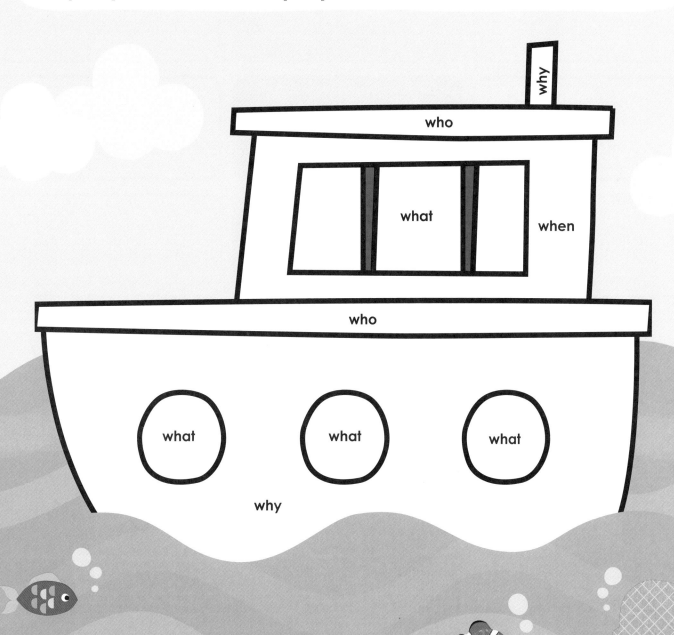

Sight words 8

Color it. Trace it. Write it.

come	come	
came	came	
some	some	
same	same	

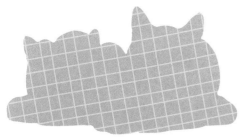

Some cats look the **same**.

	come	came	some	same
Whisper it.	come	came	some	same
Say it.	come	came	some	same
Clap it.	come	came	some	same

Word maze

Follow the word **come** to help the rocket reach the moon.

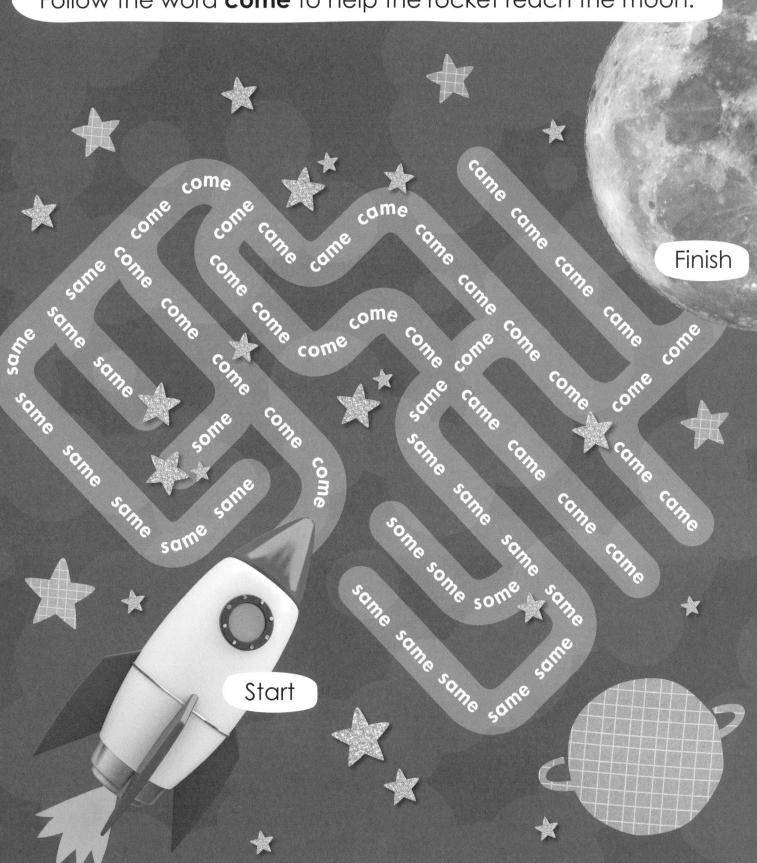

Finish

Start

Sight words 9

Color it.   Trace it.   Write it.

Color it.	Trace it.	Write it.
went	went	
away	away	
from	from	
here	here	

She **went away from here.**

Whisper it.	went	away	from	here
Say it.	went	away	from	here
Clap it.	went	away	from	here

Find the word

wint   wont   whent   went

ayaw   awey   away   awya

from   fram   fron   form

heer   nere   hare   here

Color it. Trace it. Write it.

make	make	
take	take	
where	where	
there	there	

I **make** cupcakes.

	make	take	where	there
Whisper it.	make	take	where	there
Say it.	make	take	where	there
Clap it.	make	take	where	there

Count the words

Help Tom count the words. Write the numbers in the boxes.
Circle the word that appears most often.

make ☐   take ☐   where ☐   there ☐

make where make
make take make
there make there
make make take
there there
where take
there make
make where
take where

Color it. Trace it. Write it.

did	did	
would	would	
could	could	
should	should	

I **would** if I **could**.

	did	would	could	should
Whisper it.	did	would	could	should
Say it.	did	would	could	should
Clap it.	did	would	could	should

Word search

Help Liam find each sight word in the word search.

did ✓ would ✓ could ✓ should ✓

```
w  d  e  c  o  w  s  d  d
d  i  d  l  u  o  h  e  s
w  o  u  l  d  e  o  a  h
e  l  e  o  u  i  u  i  o
u  a  b  u  i  s  l  h  l
l  c  o  u  l  d  d  d
d  m  o  d  e  o  a
a  t  s  h  o  d
```

Congratulations!

GOOD WORK AWARD!

Name: ....

has successfully completed the

Kindergarten
Sight Words Workbook.

Date: ....